Isaac S. Moses

The Profession of Judaism

Four Sermons Delivered on New Year's Eve And Morning

Isaac S. Moses

The Profession of Judaism
Four Sermons Delivered on New Year's Eve And Morning

ISBN/EAN: 9783744743488

Printed in Europe, USA, Canada, Australia, Japan

Cover: Foto ©Thomas Meinert / pixelio.de

More available books at **www.hansebooks.com**

The

Profession of Judaism.

FOUR SERMONS

Delivered on New Year's Eve. and Morning, September 18th
and 19th, and on the Eve. and Morning of the
Day of Atonement, September
27th and 28th, 1895,

BY

Isaac S. Moses,

Rabbi of Kehilath Anshe Mayriv.

CHICAGO, ILL.:
S. Ettlinger Printing Co.
1895.

DEDICATED

TO

THE MEMBERS OF KEHILATH ANSHE MAYRIV,

with Friendship and Esteem.

' Isaac S. Moses.

I

"Nil Desperandum."

Sermon for the Eve of New Year's Day.

Text: Psalm xxvii. 14.

THIS very hour a year is passing out of sight, another is coming into view. By the hallowed custom of Israel we are gathered to solemnly bid farewell to the dying year, and with prayers and songs welcome the new-born messenger of eternity. Though time and space are limitless and measureless, yet to man is given the power wherewith to set bounds to, and divide time from time, and to poise his mind in space. While the seasons wax and wane and the suns complete their cycles in never-varying monotony, man reads ever new meaning into the processes of nature, and from youth to age spells his moods into the speeding orbs. To childhood's fancy time seems endless, hours are days, and days years; to advancing manhood and womanhood time comes with quickened pace, and every changing season is an invitation to pause and to meditate, to look backward and forward ere the journey is resumed; and when the sunset glow of old age heralds the approaching night, the natal hour of a new year vibrates with forebodings of eternity. Our joys and our sorrows, our successes and our failures, our victories and our defeats, all the manifold experiences of our life, are reflected from the mirror of time.

To many of us, the past twelve months have been full of sad experiences, full of trials and visitations. Stern and harsh reality thwarted many a noble purpose and turned gladsome hope into grief and sorrowing. Many of us have seen how perishable are all earthly treasures, how frail mortal strength, how insecure is the tenure of life. Here the tender bud, the fragrant blossom, is chilled by the early rime, there the strong, fruit-bearing tree is uprooted by a passing storm. We look around about us on this night of remembrance with tear-bedimmed eyes, for many a place is vacant, many a seat is empty. With loving memory we linger on some sacred spots where, o'ershadowed by willow and monument, the dear ones sleep in eternal rest. And, oh, how many have passed through experiences compared with which death would be a welcome redeemer! "The heart knoweth the bitterness of the soul, and no stranger can share its sorrow." Few there are of maturer age who can look back upon the past year without a sigh. It has not brought the fulfilment of wishes cherished at its entrance; our prayers tonight ascend in quest of the same blessings which we craved a year ago.

This sadder mood is but natural when we contemplate the fleetness of time; but is it also reasonable? Has the past year brought us only sorrow, and not also joy? Why strike these minor chords? Why not, rather, touch the more joyous strains, and the sweeter melodies of life? "There is a soul of good in things evil," and no tear that is shed but wakes a flower to gladden our heart. This is the message of the dying year, this its parting benediction. "Remember," it says to those who sigh and groan, "the gifts I have brought, not what I have taken away." In your eager quest after happiness you have often sped by and left behind the blessings of peace, the joys of home, the ties of friendship; and now, deceived by the mirage of an Eden of delight, you imagine that before you, almost within reach, stands the Tree of Life whose fruit shall fill your soul with bliss. But the vision is deceptive and, like the horizon, it recedes at your approach. Look behind you and behold the faces of your dear ones, the eyes that beam with love for you, and give thanks to Him who guides and rules our destiny, for the untold riches, for the priceless treasures of love, of faithfulness, of friendly sympathy, for the uplifting and protecting influences by which you are surrounded. Yes, gratitude, this should be the first note in the symphony of praise with which to greet the new year. Ungrateful is he who, on the threshold of a new year, can think only of the losses he has sustained and not also remember the moments of victory, the hours of triumph. Does not every day, by the faithful fulfilment of our duty, bring to us a harvest of peace, the joy of reward? Every

earnest work, every honest endeavor, bring in
their wake a divine compensation. No victory
without battle, no triumph without sacrifice.
Tears are the dew-drops that refresh the arid soil;
loss and grief, pain and sorrow, are the seed-
germs out of which must grow the fruit of character. They know not the depth of their own soul,
nor the majesty and dignity of their manhood
and womanhood, who have never tasted of the
bitter cup of life, who have never looked into the
grim and stern face of sorrow. Let us remember the Talmudic injunction: "It is the duty of
man to thank God for evil tidings as well as for
good." Gratitude is the fragrance that sweetens
every adversity, it is the perfume of our happiness.
Thanks be to him who has preserved our lives
and the lives of our dear ones, who has surrounded
us with His mercies that from our abundance we
could relieve the sufferings of others, that we could
bring light to homes that were shrouded in darkness; thanks also for the shadows that fell across
our thresholds; thanks for the knowledge of ourselves which the past year has taught us.

And now, as we turn to welcome the new year,
another message divine sounds within our hearts:
—"Be strong and of good courage; hope thou in
the Lord." Gratitude for the past, courage for the
present. We are combatants on the battle-field of
life. To the young and to the careless, life seems
a banqueting-hall; the invited guests are welcomed
by the smiling host; pleasant conversation, delight-

ful music, tempting viands—all devices and charms
of refined taste—lend their aid to make the heart
glad, to fill the mind with joy. Real life does not
bear out this enchanting picture. To the great
multitude that people the globe, life is a fierce
struggle for existence, a continual combat. How
few are they who can live without toil, and appar-
ently pursue a path of pleasure without concern
for their daily needs ! And is not toil but another
word for struggle? It is the organized and sys-
tematized warfare of man against nature, and man
against man. No more with cruel weapons of
brutal force does the individual man face his foe,
but with the subtle and cunning devices of industry
and enterprise, with capital and contract, is the
cruel war carried on. Our civilization is the result
of a thousand forces warring against each other.
Class against class, interest against interest, nation
against nation, stand in hostile array, ready to
snatch from the competitor the bread of life. As
in physical warfare, so in all struggles and issues
of life, personal courage is the first and chiefest
element of victory. To stand firm and undismayed
amidst the terrors of death-dealing shafts; to hear
unterrified the cannon's roar, the explosion of pro-
jectiles; to behold without wincing the fall of
comrades and friends, yet all the while discharging
his duties, obeying the sound of command, unmind-
ful of the fate that may befall him—this quality of
courage marks the hero on the battle-field; and the
secret of this courage, the soul of such heroism, is
not indifference to death or danger, but enthusiasm

for duty, the firm resolve to do and to dare the
hour's bidding. Victory or defeat are only incidents, not incentives, of true heroism. In the
hard and cruel struggle of life, in the midst of a
hostile world—danger lurking at our feet, treachery
lowering over our heads,—such courage must be
the virtue to strengthen our hearts. What is
courage? The knowledge of our ability and re-
sponsibility, the consciousness of our duty to ourselves and to those dependent on our care, the
thought of honor and of honesty, the voice of our
conscience and our conviction—all these divine
impulses will make us strong and fearless, firm and
faithful in the fulfilment of our assigned task of
life. No matter how high or low the rank we fill,
how important or insignificant the post we occupy,
how great or how small the success we achieve, if
in the performance of our duty we are guided and
influenced by this voice divine, ours is the crown of
heroism, the laurel of victory. "Do thy duty, tide
what may," is the charge of this hour. The world
cannot give nor take away the soul's true greatness.
What is not within us is worthless tinsel. The
gain of the year and the years, what is it compared
with the heart's nobleness and the soul's freedom?
Though the heavens fall and the earth tremble, the
man of courage will stand erect, with eye directed
toward the polar star of duty. "I will kill thee,"
said the master to Epictítus, his slave. "Thou canst
not kill me," was the answer, "though thou mayest
choke this body." The chains of iron do not en-
slave, nor does the writ of freedom give liberty; the

courageous man alone is free, though wasting in the dungeon. To have gained this priceless gift of courage, and to take with us over the threshold of this new year the knowledge of our worth, and the consciousness of our duty, is the realization of the psalmist's promise of God's blessing: "Be strong and of good courage, for He will strengthen thy heart; hope thou in the Lord."

Yea, hope for the future. Dark, like this moon-less night, the future spreads before us. Who can tell what awaits him in the fields and valleys beyond? A step forward and he may be hurled into the abyss yawning before his very feet. While we are dreaming of coming success, we are perhaps even now caught in the net of misfortune. Our finely spun devices, our subtle speculations, and even our more cautious plans, how suddenly may they be overturned by an unforeseen event! We live today; others who have been with us, dear and near, have been unexpectedly called away. Do we know how long we shall be permitted to look into the faces of our dear ones, to rejoice in their joy, to help them in their struggles? Life, health, riches, position, the esteem of our fellow-men—how often do we see them vanish like a dream of the night? He who sets his heart on them must not repine at the dis-enchantment. Hope is spun of stronger thread than the cobwebs of vain ambition. It is the heart's power to penetrate the invisible future and read by the strong light of faith the story of its destiny. To hope means to see. This is the kinship of the word in Hebrew and in Roman tongue. This great world around us in which we live, is not a soap-bubble of chance, and human destiny not a meaningless outcome of stupid fate. Divine wisdom and divine love are the active and conscious forces in the life of matter and of man. Nothing happens, all is determined. Whatever is in harmony with the divine plan must prosper; whatever is discordant in the heavenly music must perish. If we are true to our inward voice of right, if by our toil we contribute to the triumph of justice, the dominion of love, the sovereignty of truth, we, ourselves, inscribe our names in the Book of Life, and with the eye of hope we behold the signs and promises of a higher destiny. To live, to eat, to dream, to die, these are vain endeavors. To toil for truth, to strive for wisdom and for virtue, to be a co-worker with God in shaping human character, these are no phantasms of dream-land, these are no childish longings born of desire and consumed in yearning; such hopes are anticipations of truth, fore-knowledge of eternity. Not what may happen but what, by God's will, must happen, is the vision and inspiration of true hope.

Therefore, friends, fear not, tremble not, despair not! The future can hold no terror for us: our destinies are in God's hand. He, who from multitudes of ills has saved us, through sickness and through sorrow has borne us, He will strengthen our soul, and courageously we shall take up anew our life, and cheerfully pursue its course to the goal which He has destined for us. Thus shall we be sanctified and consecrated for the year that now awaits us. Ennobled through gratitude, strengthened with courage, and uplifted by hope, we bid welcome to the new year and what it brings to us. And with Gœthe's master-song, as rendered into English sound by Carlyle's muse, we repeat:

The future hides in it
　Gladness and sorrow ;
　We press still thorough.
Naught that abides in it
Daunting us, - onward!

And solemn before us
　Veiled the dark portal ;
　Goal of all mortal :—
Stars silent o'er us
Graves under us silent.

While earnest thou gazest,
　Comes boding of terror,
　Come phantasm and error ;
Perplexing the bravest
With doubt and misgiving.

But heard are voices,
　Heard are the sages,
　The worlds and the ages :
"Choose well ; your choice is
Brief and yet endless."

"Here eyes do regard you
　In eternity's stillness ;
　Here is all fullness,
Ye brave to reward you ;
Work, and despair not!"

And to you all may the greeting in the quainter Jewish form, be my benediction :—לשנה טובה תכתבו Unto a Happy Year shall ye be written. Amen.

II

The Purpose of Life.

Morning Sermon for the New Year's Day.

Text: Deut. xxx. 15. See, I have set before thee this day life and good, and death and evil: in that I command thee this day to love the Lord, thy God, to walk in His ways and to keep His commandments. I call to witness against you this day heaven and earth, that I have set before you life and death, blessing and curse; therefore choose life.

TO CHOOSE is man's prerogative. All creatures below him must follow the bent of their nature; he alone is free to choose between right and wrong, good and evil. That we may choose life and not death, blessing and not curse, is the urgent call of the New Year's Day. Life, *life*, fuller, larger life, is the dominant note in the weird and varied melody of this day's prayers: "Remember us unto life, O thou King who delightest in life, and inscribe us in the Book of Life." But what is life? What is its meaning, what its goal? Is life but duration in time, expansion in space, or is there in all functions and faculties a purpose to be realized, an end to be reached? This is the question which each New Year's Day puts to the thoughtful. To have

added another year to the number of those that
preceded it, and, in that measure, to have come
nearer the inevitable end awaiting everything that
breathes on earth, is a thought not calculated to wake
within us sentiments of joy and gratitude. It is
different when the pulses of youth beat within us,
and the charms of existence have not yet lost their
spell. Then to breathe is pleasure, to roam about in
field and forest, on mountain peak or flower-covered
vale, is delight unspeakable. Every season is
fraught with new blessings, every year is the har-
binger of new hope. The brief past appears glori-
fied in memory's mirror; golden the future lies before us; the heart is filled with undaunted courage,
the soul beholds visions of daring deeds; grand ideals
loom up before the mind. Let us not begrudge to
swiftly passing youth this entrancing dream: soon
enough come the bitter disillusions of life.

In the whole range of nature below man the purpose of life seems clear and easily realized. When
spring-time comes the sleeping plants awake and
unfold their leaves; the flowers lift their tiny heads
toward the sun and drink in light and dew from the
heavens above; they bud and blossom and spread
their fragrance abroad; and when winter storms sweep
over the earth, they wither and die—they have
accomplished their appointed task. So all children
of nature come and go to do their Master's bidding;
they bear within themselves the law of their com-
pleteness. Man alone feels his incompleteness.
He, of all creatures, is imperfect. When the year
is done and he counts up his achievements and

his successes, what is there that is left on which his eye can dwell with satisfaction? From morn to night, from youth to age, he toils; and when the eventide of life silently and solemnly approaches, how many are there who, artist-like, can lay aside their tools and look contentedly on the work· done, and lie down to peaceful slumber? Shall we say that human life has no purpose? Shall we repeat with the cynic and the pessimist that life is an evil, existence a curse, and death the end of all? This day brings to us a more cheerful answer than barrenness and despair. The Shofar's sound wakes within us a higher thought than death and destruction. This day teaches us the meaning of the Psalmist's prayer : "Give me understanding that I may live." To live wisely and intelligently, to grow in goodness with the advancing years, and to be an instrument for good in the lives of others, to further every high endeavor, every noble enterprise, is to fill out the frame-work of our life with blessing, to endow our existence with aim and purpose.

By the inspiration of this day you will, no doubt, give assent to this definition of life. In the glare and the hurry of the daily routine, another theory prevails. For most men the purpose of life is neither intellectuality nor goodness, but enjoyment. They are painfully conscious of the brevity of existence, the insecurity of possession. With the air of superior wisdom they proclaim: "Knowledge is weariness of the soul; there is nothing better for man than to enjoy this life, and let no pleasure escape him, for there is no remembrance in the grave whither we go." The falacy of this argument becomes apparent when we test it by the capacity of human nature for enjoyment. For that nature is so constituted that the pleasures of yesterday become insipid today; the most coveted treasures lose with their novelty also their attractiveness. He who makes pleasure the object of his life soon ends by loathing it. In the ratio as we grow older, we become more indifferent to the enjoyments which in youth filled out our whole soul. The mind alone cannot be satiated. "The eye is never satisfied with seeing, nor the ear with hearing." The soul cannot be overfed; if not neglected it grows younger and stronger with increasing age. Every year must, therefore, be a step forward and upward on the road of knowledge. If we do not grow wiser as we grow older, our advancing age would testify only to decay and decrepitude; for there is no standstill neither in nature nor in man. He who does not advance, recedes, he who does not grow upward, grows downward. Years must tell not of the approaching end but of richer experience, clearer conceptions, broader views of life. Each New Year's Day not only reminds us of the fleetness of time but also of the law of our being that demands unfolding of our powers, moral growth, intellectual progress.

It is thus that the New Year's Day becomes a day of judgment; for it summons us before the court of our conscience to render account to ourselves of what we done with the time and the opportunities given us ; whether we have advanced spiritually or whether we have moved around in a circle, and are here today with the same narrowness, the same prejudices, the same hatreds which clung to us a year ago. It asks us to testify for or against ourselves whether we have become more of man and less of animal.

The way of life has often been compared to an ascent to a mountain peak. The higher we rise the purer is the air we breathe, the wider the outlook we have. The petty divisions, the little obstacles, disappear, and we look down upon a complete landscape. Having advanced in life, can you testify of yourself that you breathe a purer air intellectually? Is your heart free of unworthy desires, of degrading avarice, of mean vindictiveness? Have you acquired the habit of looking upon man and mankind with a kindly eye, striving to find in each the better and nobler trait instead of discovering their weakness, their smallness? Do you see in the struggles and toils of your fellow-beings something worthy of your sympathy and benevolence? If not, in what consists the gain of the years, the fruitage of age, the profit of life?

Our time is accustomed to estimate man by less ideal measures ; material advantage seems to be the standard of worth, and a false conception of science comes to lend emphasis to this view of life. Man is not a progressive being, but a creature of habit, it is alleged ; he can do things well only by repetition ; and the success of our civilization consists in apportioning to each man a certain limited work. To be

a successful business man one must exclude from
the range of his thought and ambition everything
that does not tend directly to further his interests;
with the regularity and punctuality of a clock he
must complete his daily work. Man is thus degraded to a machine which performs mechanically
its appointed task. Let us, for the sake of argument, make use of this simile. Man is a machine,
but there is this difference that he feels the pang of
hunger and thirst and will provide food to nourish
the body, garment to clothe it and roof to shelter it.
Without this effort on his part, the activity of the
human machine will soon come to an end. Just
think of the stupendous task of man to keep this
machinery in motion; think of the bushels of corn
and wheat to be ground and baked into bread that
he may eat; of the flocks and herds, of birds and
fishes that are to be transmuted into blood and
muscle, the sheep that must give their fleece that
he may be clothed, and all the thousandfold activi-
ties and professions brought into play, simply to
sustain life—a whole lifetime of work in order to
live! And is this all? Is there not something
missing? To eat in order to live, to live in order to
eat, is this all there is of life? Think of a
machine which would require train-loads of coal and
reservoirs of water to produce and maintain a high
pressure of steam, hundreds of skilled hands to feed,
regulate and control it, of iron arms moving forward
and backward to set in motion hundreds of wheels
driven by connecting bands; think of the din and
noise of revolving wheels, the shriek of the steam

whistle announcing the beginning and close of work,
—and then imagine that while all this is going on
the huge machinery is running empty, the finely
constructed mechanism transforming no raw material into ready fabric. Would you not declare this
machinery useless, and him who puts it in motion
to be void of sense? Let us even suppose a machine
so ingeniously constructed as to produce its own
fuel and run without human attendance, yet producing nothing else that could be converted into
value. Would you not declare this to be a profitless
undertaking? And are not the lives of most men
spent in such useless work? Feeding, *feeding*,
FEEDING, producing strength to produce again only
food and converting it into nothing else but what
will sustain animal life—can you call this life? Is
it not death, mental, moral and spiritual death? If
the human machine is to be of any value, it must
produce something else beside bread ; it must produce thought, ideas and ideals; it must produce
goodness, helpfulness, sympathy, kindness; it must
give us a rich output of love, reverence, gratitude ;
it must provide a large stock of ennobling beauty,
of uplifting melody, consoling hope ; it must tend to
give to life spiritual dignity, intellectual com-
pleteness, fullness, in a word to bring it into
harmony with the higher plan and thought of God.
But man is not intended to be a machine, he shall
rise to moral freedom and not do things by routine
and habit, but thoughtfully and advisedly, changing
methods with motives to accomplish a higher good.

It is, therefore, no mere figure of speech when

Scripture charges us to *choose* life and not death, good and not evil. Behold! both are before us. and every New Year's Day ought to rouse within us the firm determination to produce something of spiritual worth, which shall last beyond the time-limit allotted to us on earth.* To him who chooses such a life, age is, indeed, a crown of glory, and the increasing years bring a harvest of blessing: yea, blessing not only to him, but through him also to others.

No one can live for himself, independent of the lives and labors of others. However callous one may seem to be to the interests of others, he will still care for their good opinion of him, and would not like to hear himself spoken of as one utterly useless to the world, one whose demise would not in the least be felt as a loss, who would not be missed nor mourned nor kindly remembered. And so, many do some good even against their inclination, simply not to forfeit the respect of their fellow-men. We have, each of us, our natural sphere of work and usefulness, and many who do their nearest duties conscientiously do perhaps more for the blessing of the world than the professional philanthropists and noisy benefactors; because it is not merely a question of work but of usefulness. Whom have we *benefitted* by our activity, whose life has been *blest* by our endeavor, who has been made *better*, nobler, wiser, by our example and influence? this must be the measure of our work and not merely the fact that we have been doing something, or trying to do something, outside of our business interests. A close examination might reveal the unpleasant truth that, instead of a blessing we have been a curse to others, instead of helping we have been hurting their moral nature, instead of doing good we have been doing harm to lives depending upon our wisdom or wealth. Ah, we sometimes are tempted to doubt the sanity of the human intellect when we see men who by a word could make thousands happy, by a generous deed would arouse to noble emulation hundreds waiting for an example; men whose knowledge, experience and worldly means would enable them to lead the way for others in matters that must bless the living generation and those that will follow, but who will do none of these things; they let the opportunity slip by; they waste and fritter away their energies in small and worthless pursuits, born of vainglory and nourished by subbornness. And what should we think of those who, instead of increasing human happiness and raising human dignity and honor, bend their utmost to lay snares and traps for their fellowmen, to gain advantage by others' misfortune, or to enjoy the proud feeling of their own importance by wreaking vengeance for imaginary wrongs, and reveling in the unhappiness brought upon others? Is such a life-work worthy to be called human?

If there be any within this house today who have made no better use of their time and opportunities than to be a scourge to others, let the Shofar's sound arouse within their souls the sense of remorse and repentance, so that this day may become a turning-point in their lives for good; indeed the beginning not only of a new year, but of a new life, a more helpful, useful and fruitful life than the one they have led till now. Every day is a gift of grace, a new opportunity, to change the follies of youth, the failures of manhood, the fastidiousness of age into earnest, conscientious work, into strong, purposeful activity, into loving and encouraging example for the blessing, the spiritual growth of our fellow-men. Let us then avail ourselves of this new offer of time. As we pray today, "Remember us unto life," let us in the coming year so interpret it by our deeds that it may prove to be a blessing and not a curse, good and not evil, both unto us and unto those who shall be blessed through us. Amen.

III.

The Pathology of Sin.

Sermon for the Eve of the Day of Atonement.

Text: Exodus xv. 26.

THE analogy between the ills of the body and the ills of the spirit has often been pointed out; and the phrase, "A physician of the soul," is more than a happy comparison. Not only does the soul suffer when the body is racked with pain, but the reverse is true: mental suffering produces bodily illness. Care in the heart of man will bow down his physical frame; fear or remorse will shatter his nerves and undermine his health. It is no wonder that in primitive society when arts were few and the sciences undeveloped, that religion assumed the function both of priest and of physician, even as today among savage tribes the medicine-man is also the spiritual adviser. As mankind rose from savagery to civilization, division of labor lightened each toiler's work and made possible the present gigantic progress in science, art, literature, religion and government. Medicine, freed from the trammels of theology, has indeed become the deliverer of mankind from ills which a mistaken notion of religion held as the special domain of divine interference. To the physician, rather than to the priest, the modern man looks for salvation, and puts a trust in medical science far stronger than he places in the assurances of religion.

It is only very recently that a better method of treatment has been accorded to those unfortunate ones in whom the light of reason has become dimmed. Insanity is considered no more a divine visitation, or a possession by an evil spirit, but as a bodily sickness. Still wider and wider grows the sphere of medical science. It now draws within its domain the vast number of criminal phenomena, and endeavors to prove that vice, too, is a bodily disease, either by heredity, or as a form of atavism to primitive savagery. Psychology has dropped its sceptre of supremacy; physiology is the queen to whom medical science pays homage.

And yet, there are diseases which baffle the skill of the physician, maladies for which medical science has no remedy, cancerous growths which the physicist's scalpel cannot remove. Sin is a sickness that is not catalogued in the physician's hand-book; wickedness is a wound which the surgeon cannot heal; passion is a disease for which no Pasteur has yet discovered an antidote. The stricken soul can find remedy only at the hand of a physician who does not come with microscope and chemical retort, with tinctures and with toxines, but with the healing grace of divine truth. Religion is the physician whom God has sent to restore and preserve our moral health. As to ancient Israel so to us comes the divine promise: "If thou wilt listen to the voice of the Lord, thy God, and will do what is right in His sight, and wilt give ear to His commandments and keep all His statutes, all the diseases which I have brought on the Egyptians I will not bring upon thee, for I am the Lord, that healeth thee."

To no physician is given a more difficult task than awaits him who assumes to speak in the name of God, and to point out the remedy for our moral and spiritual ailments. To the sufferer in body the physician is a welcome visitor. He looks up to him with confiding trust. From his features he reads hope of recovery or tidings of despair. In most cases the patient is deeply conscious of his malady; if not of the nature and cause of his trouble, at least of the fact that he needs the physician's help. Not so is it with him in whose soul sin has found entrance, whose spirit is attacked by moral disease, whose better nature is being sapped by an evil passion. He is not conscious of any ailment, and indignantly will resent the imputation that he belongs to the morally diseased and stands in need of spiritual treatment. Like the mentally deranged, he labors under the delusion that not he, but the physician is the one who requires medical aid. If he be a man of power and influence, he will use proper measures to prevent any undue interference with his spiritual affairs; he will see to it that the officious disciple of religion be silenced and taught to know his place. But, as a true, honest and faith-

ful physician who cares for the health of the patient
more than for the fee he may receive, and will stand
abuse and taunt rather than humor the delusion of
his patient, so he who has been charged with the
solemn task of being a physician of the soul, must
speak the word of God fearlessly and truthfully,
and show not only the nature of the evil but point
out its remedy.

Scripture repeatedly refers to the diseases which
prevailed in Egypt, and from which, through obedience to the divine command, Israel may escape.
Now, what were these diseases? Had we no other
sources of information regarding ancient Egypt than
those incidents and references associated with the
story of Israel as recorded in the Bible, we would be
in a position to reconstruct or, at least, to sketch a
sufficiently distinct picture of the civilization, the
power, the wisdom and the grandeur of that ancient
empire. But of late a host of scholars have been at
work to solve the riddle of the sphinxes, to make
them tell their story. With infinite pains and
patience they have spelled into intelligent articula-
tion the tongue of the Pharaohs and have enriched
the libraries of modern nations with the valuable
literature of the dwellers of the Nile-valley. The
student is thus enabled thoroughly to understand the delicate hints of the Bible as to the diseases
of Egypt. They were many, subtle and grievous;
not without strong resemblance to the ills of our own
age. To begin with, the social structure of Egypt
was laid on the broad basis of human slavery.
This term must be taken in its broader, not its spe-

cific meaning; not merely slavery of certain individuals purchased for money or acquired through warfare, but the enslavement of the masses, the systematic oppression and exploitation of that large and broad volume of population constituting in very deed the people of the land. Society was divided into castes which it was impossible for the individual to overleap—the priesthood, the warriors, the artisans, the agriculturists, the herdsmen; all these classes were kept separate from each other as if they belonged to different nations. It is almost impossible for a modern man to measure the intensity of pride with which the upper classes looked upon the lower, and the utter disregard for the welfare and the destiny of those underneath them. The conception of a common humanity was as strange and as foreign to the minds of the ruling classes as it is a familiar truth with us. In such a social system the stranger or the foreigner could find no other place than that of abject servitude. To royalty and the ruling classes, what meaning had the word, "The right of man?" Human material was cheap; it had no other function than to serve and to be wasted in the interest, or for the glory, or the whim of those in power. Callousness and indifference to the needs and faculties of millions of human beings, gross selfishness and heartlessness in the presence of wide-spread suffering and distress, are they not evil diseases, incurable maladies, festering wounds, vitiating and poisoning the body politic?

Hand in hand with this abuse of power, and virtually an outcome of it, went the corroding and corrupting abuse of wealth, seeking satisfaction in lavish display and luxury, and in the voluptuousness of pleasure, passion and vice. Oh, the physicians of Egypt could write very interesting books for the polite society of their times, vying in subtle suggestiveness or nude realism with the literary productions of the latest French school. Culture and corruption, refinement and rottenness, were almost synonyms. Social position was a beautifully decorated garment for public wear, covering a multitude of sins that had to shun the light of day. In the higher circles of Egyptian society it betokened a lack of breeding to measure men and women by the hard and harsh rules of an antiquated morality that demanded purity, chastity, fidelity, honesty, truthfulness, justice. Such a perversion of the simplest and most natural laws of virtue could not fail to work havoc with the physical health of those noble, high-born, well-bred and correct-mannered ladies and gentlemen of the upper four hundred of Egyptian capitals. The Biblical writer undoubtedly had access to reports of very instructive and often very strange complications of clinical experience. Out of such knowledge he could well advise his simple-hearted, untutored shepherds to take heed of the manners of Egyptians, not to imitate their doings, that they may escape all the diseases that were put upon Egypt.

Another evil of Egypt was a gross abuse of religious power and organization. The priesthood of Egypt had evolved a huge and sombre theology which, like some submarine monster, spread its polypous arms over all relations of life and held in abject thralldom the minds of the people. Nowhere has the religious instinct of man produced such grotesque and abnormal shapes of worship as in the land of the Pharaohs. The deification of animals had been carried to such an unnatural degree that one might well question the sanity of minds bending in adoration before crocodile, bull or cat. But when we read of the wisdom of the ancient Egyptian priesthood; when we study their works on medicine, astronomy and geometry; when we discover that they were in possession of scientific truths which for thousands of years had been unknown to mankind, and only lately been re-discovered by the master minds of the new time, we must reject the idea of their religious insanity, and can account for that strange aberration of worship only by the assumption that the priesthood consciously and purposely cradled the public mind in gross superstition, that thereby they might retain their power and influence over the people. These sages of old said to themselves, For us wisdom, for the people ignorance; for us light, for the masses darkness; for us the joy and gladness of knowledge, for the multitude the fear and gloom of superstition. The consequence of such a position was a wide-spread and far-reaching system of hypocrisy. The expounders of religion were the most irreligious; the teachers of faith were the foremost infidels; the servants of God were the most servile of men. For hypocrisy is the mother of immorality. It creates

a double standard of rectitude, one for the public
eye, and one when secure against exposure. Hypocrisy chokes conscience and deadens self-respect. It
silences the voice of self-examination and self-
reproach. It courts public opinion and is ready to
sacrifice the truest interests of mankind to public
clamor. It worships today at the altar of fashion;
it casts into the mire the idol of yesterday. What
is honesty, truth, probity, loyalty, friendship, to
the hypocrite? He who has not the fear of God in
his heart, who does not believe in the truth which
he professes with his lips, has lost the sense of
honor; he cannot respect the honest opinions of
others, he despises the upright man and, in fact,
holds in contempt all those who strive to live a
higher life; the successful knave is his ideal man;
the brute is his God, dirt his deity, dust his goal.
Tell me of a disease which is more dangerous and
contagious than hypocrisy! It poisons the very
marrow of our moral nature and makes us incapable
of withstanding the ravages of sin, or of recovering
from the torpor of vice.

Over against these diseases of Egypt Moses constructed his great system of Israel's commonwealth, resting it on equality of human rights, on
the dignity of human life, on the sanctity of the
human soul; protesting against the enslavement of
man by brother-man; hedging the right of possession by so many precautionary measures that no
avaricious and maneuvering land-shark could swal-
low up the poor man's property; surrounding
domestic life by so many laws of purity that wealth

could tend only to the sanity not the debauchery of
the body; and teaching a God whose essence is
truth, whose garment is righteousness, and who
reveals Himself to man as the highest reason and
deepest love. The Mosaic system of religion is a
radical cure for all these social diseases. It has
proved its efficacy in the life of Israel; it has produced a people sound and strong in body and
soul, a people that could withstand and outlive the
poison of ages, the contagion of corrupt nations.
Well could this shepherd law-giver of Sinai exhort
those who had been slaves to the Egyptians, "If ye
will hearken to my commands and will obey the
statutes, and will listen to the voice of God, the
diseases of Egypt shall have no power over you, for
the God of Israel, He is thy physician."

This long exposition of the faults and foibles of
an ancient civilization may perhaps have taxed your
patience tonight, and probably you question its
relevancy to the solemn business before us. But to
him who can look away from his own personal
interests, the vision of the past holds out the mirror
of the present, and in the sins and the sufferings of
past ages he discovers the signs and tokens of the
approaching doom. "History repeats itself" is a
trite adage, but a true one. Does not our civilization show the most alarming symptoms of the evils
and the diseases of Egypt? We have fought for the
emancipation of the negro, but the enslavement of
the masses by our modern industrial system threat-
ens to become a plague worse than ever befell the

birth-place of Moses. No servitude so oppressive as
the monotonous drudgery of the modern toiler, who,
feeding the machinery of a huge system, becomes
himself only a machine, at best, a "hand" that is
hired and discharged without consideration for the
welfare, the fate, the future of his human being.
Allured by higher wages, multitudes throng the industrial centers where, by their numbers, they
depress the prices, and are cast out as so much
waste material. The economic and moral injury
wrought by the sudden discharge of large numbers
is never thought of by those who plan and direct.
A cut-throat competition, cruel and relentless as ever
was savage warfare, makes commercial life insecure and often dishonest, and robs the honest toiler
of the joy of assured and steady employment. And
the outcome of this universal slavery, this deadening
drudgery of modern industrialism? Is it greater
comfort, increased happiness, higher culture, better
morals? No. The result of all this "progress" is
the accumulation of huge fortunes in the hands of
few, of tremendous wealth under the control of a
few cunning and unscrupulous minds. Were the
history of some of the great fortunes of this country
to be written, it would be more interesting literature
than the detective stories of Conan Doyle. Wealth
has ever been the craving of men; but while in
former ages it was associated with regal power, fol-
lowed in the footsteps of the conqueror, or was a
reward of valorous deeds by a loyal nobility, it is
today solely the result of financial manipulations or
legislative corruption. Were I to choose between a

king by the grace of God and a king by the grace of
railroad bonds and stock jobbing, I would ever
prefer the crowned and sceptered ruler. The aristocracy of birth, which is also often of culture and
merit, is infinitely superior to an aristocracy of
wealth gotten in a hurry, often by unrighteous
methods, to be wastefully and sinfully spent, or to
be lavished in the purchase of titles from an effete
foreign nobility. And the consequence of this idola-
try of wealth in the higher classes is a maddening
hunger for enrichment in all strata of society below.
Corruption is the disease that eats away the vitals of
the body politic. To make as much as possible
within the brief tenure of office, is the sole ambition
of him who pretends to serve his country or his city.
Nor is the vile, dishonest, corrupt politician con-
demned and despised in the measure of his com-
mitted thefts. Public opinion applauds the
successful scoundrel and condemns only him who has
so clumsily conducted his affairs as to fall into the
toils of the law. And as it is with public honesty,
so with private virtue. The diseases of Egypt are
holding high carnival among us. To live, to live
much, to live high, to enjoy within the briefest time
as much as money can purchase, is the popular and
acknowledged theory. The old ideals are laughed at
as Sunday-school morality ; the sequel to the mar-
riage vow is played before the appreciative ears of
the divorce court. In this terrible quest for pleasure,
born of avariciousness, even the arts are degraded,
and the stage, instead of being a pulpit for the
masses, has become a panderer to vile excitement.

The heart finds no rest, the soul no peace; from pleasure to pleasure, from excitement to excitement, man rushes on, until his nervous system gives way under the terrible strain. No wonder that a writer like Max Nordau, feeling the pulse of modern society, declares it sick and sore from head to foot, diseased and degenerate.

Whence shall healing come? Are the sources of salvation dried up? Has religion ceased to be a physician of the soul? No. The angel of God comes with the same message as of old, but his voice is not heeded, he is not believed. Blinded in the chase after gold and dust, our age cannot see the beauty, cannot perceive the glory of true religion. To most people religion means profession of creed, acceptance of dogmas, performance of ceremonies, chanting of songs, singing of praises. To build gorgeous churches and to gather within their walls the most "respectable" people, is the ambition of the pious. That religion is infinitely more than wood or stone; that religion means righteousness, helpfulness, kindness, love, they cannot see. For them religion is an institution and not an inspiration; it is a convenient method and, perhaps, a cheaper one than the policeman's cudgel, to keep in check the unruly masses. With the utmost care and caution exploded theories and unintelligible doctrines are taught and traditions fostered, as if on belief in them depended man's happiness here and hereafter. They who teach and they who are taught feel in their heart of hearts the fallacy of their position; but religion is fashionable, and lends

respectability; it is a good introduction, and may
help business. What is to such men the voice of
conscience? What the fearless utterance of the man
of truth? Let the prophet take heed of his life;
let him not speak the terrible truth, they care not to
listen. Let him speak sweet things, pleasant words;
let him conjure up beauteous pictures of humanity's
greatness; let him hold up the mirror of heroic
deeds of the past, of the nobleness of lives that have
been. But let him beware of touching on the prac-
tical affairs of life, the nature of which he does not
understand; lest, if he persist, he will draw upon himself the encomium of being "unpopular"; one who
cannot win the affection of the influential members
of the church and deserves, therefore, to be kicked
out of the sphere of his work.

But, friends, if religion is to be not a mockery and
self-delusion, not a farcical show of vainglory, not
the childish display of our petulancy or stubbornness: if religion is to bring to us indeed the healing
balm of God's grace, it must enter into all and
every relationship of life; it must make our lives
pure, truthful, noble; it must take out the heart of
stone, the callous, indifferent soul and place in
its stead a heart full of sympathy with the
sufferings of others, of brotherly love and helpfulness for the needs of others; it must make us
earnest, self-respecting, conscientious men and
women who care not for the approval or disap-
proval of public opinion unless their own conscience
confirms the verdict. We must cast away the mask
of hypocrisy and self-complacency, and lay our souls

open to the influences and inspiration of religion; we must strive with all our power to be sincere with ourselves and not beguile our conscience with the pretexts and pretences of conventionality. And, above all, we, ourselves, must become servants and helpers of religion to cure mankind of its social and moral diseases.

One of the most distressing maladies of modern times is pauperism. It is a product of our industrial system; it follows in the wake of our prosperity as shadow follows light. Let us not deceive ourselves by the pleasing compliment to our charitable nature that occasionally we give alms to the poor. The crumb of pity thrown away from the table of plenty, is no charity. True charity means helpfulness to lift up the fallen brother and put him in a position to be self-supporting. Are we doing our full share of our obligation to the poor?—we who through good and evil times have never missed any of the necessities of life, we for whom no wind bloweth but bringeth some good— let them who can, answer in the affirmative. As a community, we have not. To us Israelites has fallen a double share of duty. We pride ourselves that we care for our own poor. How do we care for them? That is the question. Poverty is a sickness of the social body. The sick must be cured, not pampered and not abused. If your brother be sick, will you reproach him? Will you holler at him? But if our poor brother comes with pitiful mien, asking for assistance, we have cruel rebuke

and little help for him. The contributions to our
United Hebrew Charities are so utterly inadequate
to the demand made upon our office that the very
help we extend becomes a new source of irritation.
When year after year the most urgent appeal is
made for larger contributions, it is only a few who
respond handsomely—by no · means generously.
The vast majority of the better situated turn a deaf
ear to all entreaties; they shirk their duty, and with
the paltry sum which they subscribe, they pose
before the world as benefactors. Some have even
succeeded in working up a reputation for being
charitable. Years ago, when but moderately pros-
perous, they had a heart for suffering humanity;
they gave generously, even out of proportion to
their wealth. Now God has blessed them in such
a measure they hardly know how rich they are, they
have become suspicious of the claims of the poor,
and consider every appeal for help as a design to
rob them. Still they walk about with the com-
placency of saints, and ease their conscience by the
memory of their past generous acts. Or, perhaps,
they contemplate doing some good in the distant
future—when they shall have no use or opportunity
for the means at their disposal. The hungry and
naked must be fed and clothed now, and not a generation hence; the sick and the suffering must be
cared for now, and not when they shall be nó more
on earth. To refuse aid when it is in our power to
give it, to shut our heart against the pitiful cry of
the unfortunate, to thwart by our niggardliness
every thorough, systematic, radical cure of pauper-

ism in our midst, betokens a depraved nature, a
morally diseased and degenerate soul, insensible to
the touch of humanity.

By the beautiful and hallowed custom of this
community, the annual collection for the United
Hebrew Charity Association will now be taken.
Let me this time not have made a vain appeal.
Gauge your contributions not by the example of
your neighbor, but according to the measure in
which God has blessed you, and by the dictates of
your conscience do your full duty. Of such large-
hearted, wisely administered benevolence, the
Scriptural phrase is true: "Charity delivereth from
death." Yea, it delivers from the death of meanness
and heartlessness. It is the voice of God speaking
to us; it is the angel bringing the healing draught to
suffering mankind. Let such charity be yours tonight. Then will the gracious promises of Holy
Writ be fulfilled: "None of the diseases which I
have brought upon the Egyptians will I bring upon
thee, for I am the Lord who healeth thee." Amen.

IV.

The Profession of Judaism.

Morning Sermon for the Day of Atonement.

Text: Deut. x. 12.

IT is with considerable misgiving that I approach
the subject of my discourse this morning. I
desire to speak of Judaism, its nature, the reasons
we have for maintaining it. What is Judaism?
What are its requirements? What our duties to it?
Is there a more befitting theme for us to discuss on
the Day of Atonement than this? And yet I fear
that I am somewhat out of touch with my audience
in selecting Judaism for a subject. I am well aware
of the fact that with Jews Judaism is not a fashionable subject. They are not over-fond of the name
"Jew." They are not given to discussing religious
topics, least of all one which concerns them most.
Nor do they require or expect the minister in their
pulpit to call their attention to the stern, inevitable
and, withal, not altogether pleasant fact of their
being Jews. Still, if I rightly understand my position and the name of my office to be a Rabbi in
Israel, I feel it my bounden duty to at least once a

year, when I have the pleasure of seeing you all before me, bring near to your hearts the reasons why we should remain faithful and loyal to the religion which we call Judaism.

It is not a very pleasant experience to be told, often with a sneer, that no one exactly knows what Judaism is. The term is surrounded by a haze, an indefiniteness, that puzzles even the scholars and the students of religion, if required to define with exactness the line of demarcation that divides off Jew from non-Jew. Were we to ask the large majority of the civilized world, the preachers, teachers and professors of the creed by which we are surrounded, what Judaism is, the answer would not long be wanting. "Judaism," they would say, "is the religion of the Old Testament: Christianity that of the New. Judaism is the old dispensation; Christianity is the new covenant. Judaism is the religion of law and ceremonies: Christianity is the religion of love. The Jew believes in the Great Jehovah, the awful, angry God, who revealed Himself amidst the thunder and lightning of Sinai, and gave to the people of Israel a number of laws, promising His protection as long as they would keep these laws, and threatening dire vengeance and destruction if they should venture to abandon or to change them. These laws," they will tell us, "were only tentative, they were meant as an education of the people for a higher stage; they were only a preparation for a faith that was to come. It was a torch that should guide in the wilderness until the larger light would arise to illumine the world."

Judaism was only a preparation for Christianity. This having come, the old dispensation was made superfluous and ought to have vanished 1800 years ago. All of it which has not disappeared is merely a survival not of the fittest, rather the unfittest, form of religion. It clings to the poor, misguided, self-deluded Jews like a hereditary disease. It follows them from land to land, and from nation to nation. It singles them out as belonging to a peculiar people. It makes them exclusive, narrow and, to a certain extent, proud of their past, and disables them from amalgamating with, and assimilating the larger religious life that is moving all about them. Judaism is an anachronism; it is out of date and place in the modern intellectual world. Strenuous efforts have been made, and are continually made, to persuade the Jew to give up his old-fashioned, worn-out kind of religion. That he is unwilling to do so, and, despite the disadvantages it brings to him, despite prejudice and persecution that it draws upon him, he still continues to cling to this time-beaten form of faith, is evidence of something more than obstinacy and stubbornness on his part. As a class the Jews, both by heredity and by training, are mentally alert, quick to see the fallacy of a position that cannot stand the test of reason, and are not easily held in moral or spiritual subjection. If, therefore, the Jew persists in holding fast to a religious system which is declared to be superceded by a new dispensation, he must have cogent reasons for doing so. These may not be always clear to his consciousness; they may be latent, dormant in his mind, or cluster around his affections and emotions. It ought, therefore, to be of the utmost importance to us to make clear to ourselves these reasons for our adherence to Judaism.

Were we to ask a number of Israelites to give us a definition of their faith, we would receive as many different answers as there were persons to whom the query was addressed. You know there are various shades of Judaism. I do not know to which of the different forms of Jewish faith you adhere. Probably you never trouble your minds, nor give any serious thought to these matters. Let us ask a staunch orthodox Jew to tell us what his Judaism is. If he does not belong to the ignorant, uncultured class—of whom we have quite a superfluity in our midst—he will tell us, that Judaism is the covenant of God with Israel, made first with Abraham, repeated with Isaac, confirmed with Jacob and completed on Mount Sinai; that the Torah, or the law of Moses, is the unchanging and unchangeable constitution of the Hebrew people; that on the basis of it they built up a commonwealth, established themselves in a land of their own, with judges, kings and prophets, with a consecrated priesthood and a national sanctuary; that all subsequent literature was simply an amplification of the Mosaic code, that the laws and enactments of the rabbis as laid down in the Talmud and the later casuistic literature, are the outflow of the Mosaic spirit, and are binding on all Israel, and that to deny, or neglect them implies denial or rejection of Judaism. Through the destruction of the Temple and the collapse of the State, Israel's political life has not been annihilated ; it is only in suspense, and will, at the gracious time known by God, be revived in its pristine beauty and glory. The Messiah, the son of David, will lead the dispersed of Judah back to their country, and re-establish the kingdom of Israel on Palestine's soil. Whether this is your faith or not, I am unable to determine; perhaps it is, and you know it not. I shall not indulge, however tempting the opportunity, in argument to refute this position.

For me Judaism is not a polity but a faith, not a contract or covenant, but a living inspiration, not a survival or tradition but a development and continual growth of an original thought. However misunderstood by the outside world, however caricatured by many within the fold—Judaism is neither stepping-stone or foil for Christianity, nor is it racial distinctiveness and national pride, clustering around bygone glories and shattered dynasties. Judaism is a *spiritual force*, a *moral movement*, a *social mission*. It came into this world not as an invention of priests, not as a policy of kings, but as a moral guide, a spiritual illumination.

The difficulty in understanding and defining Judaism does not lie in any mystery inconceivable and unfathomable, but in its very simplicity. Because Judaism is a growth, and not an invention, because it is life, and not theory, it requires a different measurement than dogmatic faiths sprung upon the world to meet a temporary need. We need not go far in search of a definition of Judaism. The

Master-Builder who erected the magnificent system
of Israel's religion, has given us also the key wherewith to open the portals and to enter the sanctuary.
Listen to the words of the Great Teacher, the foremost of all prophets, and you will receive the de-
sired information,

"And know, O Israel, what doth the Lord
require of thee, but to fear the Lord, thy
God, to walk in His ways; and to love Him,
and to serve Him with all thy heart and all thy
soul."

These are the elements of true religion, these the
essential requirements of Judaism. To know a religion we must examine the three great divisions of
which it is composed and which have here been in-
dicated: *Reverence, Love* and *Service*. We may
translate these theological designations into terms
with which the modern thinker is more familiar:
Philosophy, Ethics and *Humanity*.

Before the tribunal of modern criticism every
religion claiming the affection of the men and women
of our age, must render account of itself and prove
its justification. It is especially necessary and
wholesome for those who entertain the high hope
that their faith is destined to be the universal faith
of mankind, shall be sure that their religion can
pass muster.

As to the philosophy of Judaism, it is contained
in its God-idea, in its spiritual attitude to the
universe. The charge that is often made by Christian
thinkers against Jewish theology is that of its
extreme poverty and fewness of thoughts. With

some ancient Greek philosophers modern theologians assert, that the Jewish mind was unable to rise above the thought of one God. The Aryan mind was more prolific, and peopled the heavens with armies of deities. Christianity reduced them to a trinity. It fructified and deepened the barren monotheism of the Jews by bringing God in human shape nearer to the heart of man. And yet, whoever follows the currents of thought as they flow through history, whoever watches the intellectual struggles of today, cannot fail to notice that the battle of modern theology rages around those very doctrines that are so proudly placed in opposition to the Jewish thought; that despite the alleged closer kinship with human nature, the dogmas of the trinity, the incarnate God, the vicarious atonement, are more and more abandoned by the intellectual portion of Christianity, and that the highest Christian thought as represented by its great thinkers, poets and writers, runs in the direction of Hebrew monotheism. The literature of today in the lands of modern civilization, in Germany, France, England, America, betrays but feeble affinity to trinitarian theology. It is saturated with the Hebrew conception of the One God, who is Father of all men. And today science comes to corroboate this ancient view. There is no room in this universe for more than one spiritual force. Unity is the principle underlying the whole cosmic order: unity the purpose of all human development. "If I were asked," says Zangwell in his famous essay on the "Position of Judaism," "If I were asked to sum up in one broad generalization the intellectual tendency of Israel, I should say that it was a tendency to unification. The unity of God, which is the declaration of the dying Israelite, is but the theological expression of this tendency. The Jewish mind runs to unity by an instinct as harmonious as the Greek's sense of art. It is always impelled to a synthetic perception of the whole. This is Israel's contribution to the world, his vision of existence. There is one God who unifies the cosmos, and one people to reveal Him, and one creed to which all the world will come. In science the Jewish instinct, expressing itself, for example, through Spinoza, who seeks for "One God, one Law, one Element:" in æsthetics it identifies the true and the beautiful with the good ; in politics it will not divide the Church from State, nor secular history from religious: for Israel's national joys and sorrows are at once incorporated in his religion, giving rise to feasts and fasts ; in ethics it will not sunder soul from body: it will not set this life against the next; this world against another; even in theology it will not altogether sunder God from the humors of existence, from the comedy which leavens the creation. *Unitas, unitas, omnia unitas.*

Will the world ever outgrow this conception of God? Or will science substitute for it an impersonal, unconscious force guiding and directing the life and destiny of man? As the human mind is constituted, we can conceive of no higher view of the principle of cause and effect than the Jewish postulate : One God, the Creator of all. Before this God of the universe the mind bends in adoration, for it feels its kinship with Him. It knows itself to be a part of this great life of God. For this God, so Judaism teaches, is not an abstraction dwelling in some remote part of the universe; His temple the human mind; His sanctuary the human heart; His seat of glory the soul of man. No inseparable gulf yawns between God and man: God the Creator, man the creature; God the Father, man the child; God the King and Sovereign, man the subject and servant. "God dwelling in man," what does it mean? It means to make man's life divine, to lift from the dust the lowly, to crown him prince of creation; it sanctifies his life by making it a part of the divine life, and thus blending dust with Deity plant heaven on the earth. In a word, God revealing Himself to man in order that man may lead a moral life. Ethics is the purpose of religion— sanctity the outcome of the fear of God.

Every religion is judged by its code of ethics. Israel need not fear to stand this test, for if sifted to its very root, Judaism is by its very nature an ethical movement. It sprang into existence in opposition to the immoral practices of the religions around it. The very first call to Abraham and the promise that he shall be a blessing, is based on the assurance that he will teach the way of God to his children and to his household, to do justice and righteousness. What are the requirements of true religion? asks the Psalmist: "Who shall ascend the hill of the Lord, who shall stand in His holy place? He who has clean hands and a pure heart." Or listen to the Prophet's creed, "Wherewith shall I come before the Lord? bow myself before the Most High? He has told thee, O man, what is good, and what God requires of thee: to do justly, to love virtue, to walk humbly with thy God. "

Study the history of Israel. The stages of his growth are the mile-stones of his moral development: intertwined and interwoven with his political life is the growth of his ethical ideas. Even his ceremonial laws and precepts were but symbolical of moral obligation. The morality of Judaism has often been contrasted with that of Christianity and declared to be on a lower level, and resting on selfish motives. If there be traces in the Old Testament and Talmudic teachings of a doctrine that makes reward the incentive of a moral act, the whole life of Israel is a refutation of this charge. For a whole nation, during hundreds of years, to pursue a path of duty in the face of almost insurmountable difficulties, to bear the persecution of the world and suffer unparalleled martyrdom, does not betray a selfish nature swayed by mercenary motives. The love of God and the love of virtue did not bring to the Jew the compensation craved and promised.

For, let it be remembered that the rewards mentioned in the Old Testament have reference to this life on earth only, to temporal happiness and wellbeing, to the permanence of national life: there is no allusion to celestial rewards, to heavenly banquets, enlivened by angelic music. Yet in the face of facts, what were the rewards of the Jew for his faithfulness and his virtue? If he did not crave heaven, he certainly did not win the earth; the joys and pleasures of the world were not his share. Nor is the charge of inadequate morality true even if judged by the current of his literature. The present generation of high-minded Christians would declare it a misstatement of facts were their morality to be judged by the standard of the New Testament only, or by the practices of the mediæval church. They claim progress, not only in thought, but also in morals. Does not the same law hold good for us? Has Israel not progressed ethically as well as intellectually since the last two thousand years? The Talmud, that oft maligned book, is full of passages breathing the most unselfish morality:—"Be not like hired servants that work for reward. Be, rather, like slaves that serve their master without thought of compensation." And another rabbi said,—"The reward of a good deed is another good deed, and one virtue brings another in its wake: and the punishment of sin is sin." Is this not a higher standard of virtue than the leering glance toward a crown in heaven? To do good because God commanded it, is a nobler incentive than to do God's command in order to save one's soul. Whether the soul of man is immortal or not, is a matter of theological speculation and faith : with the Jew it never enters as a motive of morality. As God is merciful and kind to His creatures out of His infinite love and compassion for them, so must man fulfil the moral behest out of his deep love for God—for God's

sake, and not for his own sake,—neither here nor
hereafter,—shall man love virtue and practice
it. This theory of ethics has been fully ex-
emplified in the life of Israel. His morality
has not been closed up in a book and read
as devotional literature on the Sabbath Day
while the week days testify to a different system ; but his whole life was permeated by the
feeling· of moral obligation, to do the will of his
Heavenly Father. That will is a righteous, just and
holy one, which does not demand of man anything
that is unreasonable, unjust or unholy.

And what is the purpose, the aim and goal of this
morality? What the higher plan of Israel's holi-
ness? Does obedience to the will of God and carry-
ing out His behests close the circle of man's duties?
No one who is acquainted with the history and
literature of Israel will charge him with such narrow
view. As to Abraham, so to the whole people, the
promise applies—"I shall bless thee in order that
thou shalt become a blessing." The moral life of
Israel, his entire ethical code—yea, his whole history,—it is a preparation, yet not a preparation for
Christianity, but for Humanity. The way out of
Judaism leads not into any sectarian faith, but into
a larger life which includes all men and all faiths.
And here we strike the major key of Israel's Mission
—"Israel, The servant of God," means "Israel the
servant of humanity." The theme, "The Mission
of Israel" has often been derided and ridiculed as the
presumption of arrogance, the vaunt of impotence.

If it be possible to represent to our minds the history of mankind without the presence of Israel and the contribution which this people has made to the wealth of the world ; if it is possible to construe the course of events in a manner as to leave out the currents and influences emanating from Palestine : it certainly transcends human imagination to picture the state of society today depleted of the spiritual and moral elements derived from the treasury of Israel's thought. If the Jew had rendered to the world no other service than to have given it that great book, the Bible, written with his heart blood, punctuated with his great national experiences, emphasized by the soul-hunger of his noblest sons, and sealed in the dungeon and on the scaffold with the last breath of the dying martyr—this alone would entitle him to the gratitude of all coming generations. But he has done more. He has given to civilized nations two religions which have become sources of salvation, remodeling their national character. For in this lies his secret of strength, that Israel is more than a religion, more than a theological system, that it is a *social force*, a national corrective. If Feuerbach's dictum be true, that all religion is Anthropology (that is, the study of man), it is still more so in regard to Judaism. It is not only Anthropology, it is Sociology. It is an attempt, and a successful attempt, to regulate the relation of man to brother-man, of nation to nation. That all men are born equal; that they stand on a level before God and before the civil law; that they ought to have an equal share and opportunity

in the field of toil; that high and low, rich and poor,
learned and ignorant, priest and layman, stand in
the closest inter-relation and inter-dependence with
one another, and are equally accountable for their
actions before the moral law; in a word, a Common
Humanity,—this truth did not wait for the eigh-
teenth century savants to announce it to the world;
it was the foundation of Israel's commonwealth,
the life principle in Israel's history. It made
possible the survival of the Jewish people during
centuries of persecution. His very suffering for
the sake of liberty of conscience, his frugality,
his thrift, his commercial circumspection, his
inter-nationalism, his freedom from theological
bias and dogmatic bickering, made him a valuable
instrument in the service of mankind, enabled him
everywhere to become the teacher and the inspirer
of a larger and broader society than existed around
about him. Is it mere accident that during the
middle ages, up to within recent time, the Jews were
the bankers, the physicians and often the states-
men of Christian and Mohammedan nations;
that Jewish philosophers in the persons of Ibn
Gabirol, Maimonides, Spinoza, Mendelsohn, gave
impetus to new thought; that Marx and La
Salle, both Jews, were the fathers of modern social-
ism; and that the latest Religio-Ethical movement
has been inaugurated by a Rabbi's son? The
most powerful book of today, the latest addition to
sociological literature, is the product of the Jew,
Max Nordau. This seems to be the tendency and
the drift of the Jewish mind—the prophetic spirit of

old revived in the latest descendants, seeking to
readjust and rearrange the distorted relations between man and man. If out of the chaos and con-
fusion of the present, there should arise a new form of
faith that shall offer to mankind the bread of life and
the water of health, that new form will not deny its
origin; it will bear in form and features the sem-
blance to Israel, its parent. Israel, the Servant of
God, Israel, the Servant of Humanity, is yet to
become the Messiah of mankind, bringing the new
message of social regeneration, of moral re-birth,
of spiritual unity.

Will you now ask: What is Judaism? Is it
race? Is it ritual? Is it feast or fast? Is it lan-
guage, dead or living? Is it orthodoxy, reform or
radicalism? Away with all these petty distinctions,
these belittling divisions! Rise to the height of
prophetic outlook. Judaism is Reverence for God,
Love of Virtue, Service of Humanity. Are you
ashamed of such a religion? Will you hold in light
esteem the name that binds you to such a faith?
Shame on the coward and the craven that forsakes
the flag which has witnessed these glorious battles
in the service of God and man! No more precious
heirloom can you bequeath to your children and
children's children than this honorable name "Jew!"
Live up to your faith, sanctify by your life the
name of the God whom you profess and who, through
you and your history, has been working for the
salvation of mankind. Yea, help to bring nearer
the time when the barriers will fall, and divisions
will be removed, when there will be no distinction

between Jew and non-Jew, but all men be known
and recognized as children of God, exclaiming
with us the inspiring words of our confession:
"Hear, O Israel, thy God is my God, thy people
is my people. Hear, O Israel, the Eternal is our
God, the Eternal is One." Amen.

www.ingramcontent.com/pod-product-compliance
Lightning Source LLC
Chambersburg PA
CBHW022037080426
42733CB00007B/864